*Objectivity in*
*Social Research*

Also by Gunnar Myrdal

Asian Drama: An Inquiry into the Poverty of Nations

Challenge to Affluence

Beyond the Welfare State

Economic Theory and Under-Developed Regions
  (*American title:* Rich Lands and Poor)

An International Economy, Problems and Prospects

Development and Under-Development, The Mechanism
  of National and International Inequality

The Political Element in the Development
  of Economic Theory

An American Dilemma: The Negro Problem and
  Modern Democracy

Value in Social Theory

# Objectivity in Social Research

## Gunnar Myrdal

WESLEYAN UNIVERSITY PRESS
Middletown, Connecticut

All inquiries and permissions requests should be addressed to the
Publisher, Wesleyan University Press, 110 Mt. Vernon Street,
Middletown, Connecticut 06457

Distributed by Harper & Row, Publishers, Keystone Industrial
Park, Scranton, Pennsylvania 18512

This book was first published in the United States by Pantheon
Books, a division of Random House, Inc., New York, and in
Canada by Random House of Canada Limited, Toronto.
The original publisher in the United Kingdom was Gerald
Duckworth & Company, Inc.

The text of *Objectivity in Social Research* was the 1967 Wimmer
Lecture at St. Vincent College, Latrobe, Pennsylvania.

Manufactured in the United States of America
First Wesleyan Paperback Edition, 1983

# CONTENTS

*Objectivity in*
*Social Research*

# I · *The Problem*

The ethos of social science is the search for "objective" truth. The faith of the student is his conviction that truth is wholesome and that illusions are damaging, especially opportunistic ones. He seeks "realism," a term which in one of its meanings denotes an "objective" view of reality.

The most fundamental methodological problems facing the social scientist are therefore, what is objectivity, and how can the student attain objectivity in trying to find out the facts and the causal relationships between facts? How can a biased view be avoided? More specifically, how can the student of social problems liberate himself from (1) the powerful heritage of earlier writings in his field of inquiry, ordinarily containing normative and teleological notions inherited from past generations and founded upon the meta-

physical moral philosophies of natural law and utilitarianism from which all our social and economic
theories have branched off; (2) the influences of
the entire cultural, social, economic, and political milieu
of the society where he lives, works, and earns his living and his status; and (3) the influence stemming
from his own personality, as molded not only by tra-
ditions and environment but also by his individual
history, constitution, and inclinations?

The social scientist faces the further problem: how
can he be in this sense objective and, at the same time,
practical? What is the relation between wanting to
understand and wanting to change society? How can
the search for true knowledge be combined with moral
and political valuations? How can truth be related to
ideals?

In our profession there is a lack of awareness even
today that, in searching for truth, the student, like
all human beings whatever they try to accomplish,
is influenced by tradition, by his environment, and
by his personality. Further, there is an irrational taboo
against discussing this lack of awareness. It is astonishing that this taboo is commonly respected, leaving the
social scientist in naïveté about what he is doing. To
destroy this naïveté should be the object of the sociology
of science and scientists, the least developed branch of
social science.[1] This is important, as these influences, if

1. Gunnar Myrdal, *Asian Drama. An Inquiry Into the Poverty of
Nations* (New York, Twentieth Century Fund and Pantheon Books,
1968), Prologue, Sec. 1, pp. 5–8. Unless designated otherwise all of
the references in the following are to my own works.

they are not controlled, are apt to cause systematic biases in research and thus lead to faulty knowledge.

Even if the influences conditioning research had already been exposed, so that the social scientist was more sophisticated about himself and his attitudes in searching for truth, there would still remain a problem of the philosophy of social science: are there logical means by which he can better assure objectivity in his research? This is the problem I shall lead up to in this essay.

As we shall find, the logical means available for protecting ourselves from biases are broadly these: to raise the valuations actually determining our theoretical as well as our practical[2] research to full awareness, to scrutinize them from the point of view of relevance, significance, and feasibility in the society under study, to transform them into specific value premises for research, and to determine approach and define concepts in terms of a set of value premises which have been explicitly stated.

2. I am using the words "theoretical" and "practical" (or "political") with the meanings they have in philosophy: the former refers to thinking in terms of causes and effects, the latter to thinking in terms of means and ends.

# II · *A Personal Note*

These thoughts are not universally accepted. On the contrary, the methodology of social science is for the most part metaphysical and pseudo-objective. So it may not be entirely beside the point—and may not appear unduly self-centered—to sketch heuristically the route one individual student has traveled in reaching them. Doing this was, indeed, implied in the invitation directed to me when preparing the lecture of which the present text is a revised version.

The questions formulated at the very beginning of this essay have disturbed and excited me ever since my first youthful attempts to do economic research. This I ascribe to my reaction—negative as well as positive—to the truly exceptional group of economists in Sweden of the generation before me and above me, including Knut Wicksell, David Davidson, Gustav Cassel, and Eli F. Heckscher. They combined extraordinary ability—and, of course, status in the academic republic of the world—with an equally extraordinary degree of naïveté in regard to the fundamental methodological problems I have posed.[3]

They had their spiritual roots in the late Victorian era and felt no inhibitions in arriving at definite practical and political conclusions in their research. These, they believed, expressed objective truth.

These conclusions, reached without specific and explicit value premises, were broadly of the *laissez-faire* variety (in part, Wicksell was in this respect an exception, but he passed away earlier). Like most economists of my generation in Sweden, I had different views on policy. To begin with, we were of an interventionist mind. We wanted, for instance, to plan public action in order to mitigate the widespread unemployment during the depression after the end of the First World War. We had, then, to refute our elders.

As my interest in truth-seeking was as strong as my interest in social reform, I felt an urge to liberate

3. I have attempted to describe the exceptionally stimulating milieu for young economists in Sweden after the First World War in *Value in Social Theory: A Selection of Essays on Methodology,* Paul Streeten, ed. (New York, Harper & Row, Publishers, Inc., 1958 [London, Routledge & Kegan Paul, Ltd., 1956]), Postscript, pp. 237–62 (page references are to the American edition). See also my obituary of Gustav Cassel, "Gustav Cassel in Memoriam (1866–1945)," reprinted in *Bulletin of the Oxford University Institute of Statistics,* Vol. 25, No. 1 (1963), pp. 1–10; originally in *Ekonomisk Revy,* Vol. 2, No. 1 (February, 1945), pp. 3–13.

my thinking from the fetters of the dominant tradition. In time this would take me into much wider methodological problems than those immediately relevant to the controversies in my homeland at that particular time. In those days the stern Swedish philosopher Axel Hägerström exerted a strong influence in a critical direction on the academic youth in Sweden and strengthened my critical attitude to all types of thinking in terms of objective values. My second major work[4] was originally planned as merely a brief, polemical pamphlet demonstrating the self-deception of my older colleagues in Sweden as they managed to come to policy conclusions directly from their attempts to establish the facts and factual relationships. Instead, however, it became an analysis in some depth of the way in which economic theory had branched out from the metaphysical philosophies mentioned above and of the way in which it had retained that legacy in all its various branches and particularly in its value and welfare theories—indeed, it has retained this heritage even today.

As a critique of economic theory, the thoughts expressed in that book demonstrate the economists' systematic endeavor to solve practical and political problems with one equation missing, thus leaving the door open to arbitrariness and biases. As such a critique, I believe, those thoughts are still valid—and

4. *The Political Element in the Development of Economic Theory* (Cambridge, Harvard University Press, 1965 [London, Routledge & Kegan Paul Ltd., 1953; originally published in Stockholm as *Vetenskap och politik i nationalekonomin,* 1930]).

also still relevant. Not much has changed in the thinking habits of economists. But throughout the argumentation in the book there lurked the idea that, if all metaphysical elements were radically cut away and no policy conclusions were drawn, a healthy body of positive economic theory would remain, altogether independent of valuations. It should then be possible simply to infer policy conclusions by adding a chosen set of stated value premises to the objective scientific knowledge of the facts.

This implicit belief in the existence of a body of scientific knowledge acquired independently of all valuations I soon found to be naïve empiricism. "Facts do not organize themselves into concepts and theories just by being looked at; indeed, except within the framework of concepts and theories, there are no scientific facts but only chaos. There is an inescapable *a priori* element in all scientific work. Questions must be asked before answers can be given. The questions are all expressions of our interest in the world; they are at bottom valuations. Valuations are thus necessarily involved already at the stage when we observe facts and carry on theoretical analysis, and not only at the stage when we draw political inferences from facts and valuations."[5] That early contribution to the discussion of the value problem in economics, therefore, became only a stepping stone in the develop-

5. *The Political Element in the Development of Economic Theory,* Preface to the English [language] Edition, pp. ix–xvi.

ment of my thoughts about the question I raised at the outset of this essay.

My early interests had been in economic problems and were focused on economic theory of the established type as it had developed in the classical and neoclassical tradition. Later research interests led me further and further away from that limited area until I became accustomed to thinking of myself as a political economist and, later, as an institutional economist. This was partly the result of a change in the type of practical and theoretical problems with which I became involved during my working life. On a more fundamental level these later research experiences furnished a deeper reason, which expressed itself in a growing disrespect for the traditionally rigid boundary lines between separate disciplines of social science as they have developed pragmatically to fit teaching purposes and to meet the need for specialization.

The rationale for this disrespect was my growing recognition of the fact that *in reality there are not economic, sociological, or psychological problems, but simply problems, and that as a rule they are complex*. The one and only type of concept that it is permissible to keep vague is the meaning of terms such as economics, sociology, psychology, or history since no scientific inference can ever depend on their definitions. This point, as we know, is not always acknowledged even today but was admitted still less forty years ago. In those days labor was often wasted on finding the precise definition of one or another of our several social science disciplines in the belief that this was an important activity.

We will have to master the complex problems that exist in reality by whatever tools are available. This should not be taken as an excuse for dilettantism: it is our duty to develop our skills to the highest possible degree in order to solve the scientific problems before us. The student must try to improve and adapt his skills to suit the particular problem he is tackling; he must not be content to limit them narrowly to one of the traditional disciplines. In my own professional life I have sometimes wandered far from what is usually considered economic theory, my original playground.

As I carried along with me my concern about the problem of methodology and valuations, it became related to social science broadly and not merely to economics where it had originated. Wherever I came to work, this problem raised its head, as is indicated by prologues, appendices, sections, or whole chapters devoted to it and my way of tackling it.[6] I could almost say with Mohandas Gandhi, though in a very different sense, that all my working life has been a series of "experiments with truth."

6. An incomplete collection of them, together with a few specialized articles and papers, written after the original Swedish edition of *The Political Element in the Development of Economic Theory* (1930) but before *Rich Lands and Poor: The Road to World Prosperity*, Ruth Nanda Anshen, ed. (New York, Harper & Row, Publishers, Inc., 1958) [published in Great Britain as *Economic Theory and Underdeveloped Regions*, London, Gerald Duckworth & Co., Ltd., 1957] and *Asian Drama* (1968), is contained in *Value in Social Theory*.

When I was invited to give the 1967 Wimmer Lecture at St. Vincent College, it was suggested that I should use the occasion to give a brief and simplified account of the conclusions I have reached on the problem of dealing with valuations in social research. I was also asked to account for the way in which I have reached these conclusions through various research experiences. I welcomed this opportunity and these suggestions.

The lecture has later been enlarged considerably for publication, but the text is still very compressed and simplified. I am addressing myself to an audience of students who must find it difficult and in any case laborious to have to piece together a consistent and comprehensive philosophy of social science from numerous bits and pieces scattered about in writings on all sorts of specific problems. When I feel that there might be need for a fuller treatment of a particular point, I shall indicate where it can be found. The nature of the task of providing a guide to my own thoughts over the years explains and, I hope, will excuse the fact that I have kept the references almost exclusively to my own writings.

My ambition in writing this little book has thus been to produce a text to which students in social science, including history—and perhaps also law, theology, and philosophy—can be referred and which is so brief and easy to understand that it does not take more than a minimum of their valuable time. My hope, however, has been that at least some of my young

readers might be put on the track of deeper explora-
tion into the problem and might come to challenge
much of what is in the textbooks and then see new
horizons for research.

# III · *Valuations, Beliefs, and Opinions*

As science is nothing but highly sophisticated common sense, we might most usefully start our inquiry by attempting to characterize the world outlook of ordinary people in our society—not excluding social scientists themselves when they form notions about things, both outside their branch of study and, as we shall find, even within it. In our type of civilization people in general, not only social scientists, do want to be rational and to have reasons for the ways in which they conceive of and react to the reality around them.[7]

7. What is said in this and the following three sections is developed more fully in *An American Dilemma. The Negro Problem and Modern Democracy* (New York, Harper & Row, Publishers, Inc., 1944), Introduction, Secs. 1 and 2, pp. xli–xlvii, and Apps. 1 and 10, pp. 1027–34 and 1136–43 (*Value in Social Theory*, Ch. 5, pp. 71–86).

There are two types of conception held by people about reality: in their pure form I call these *"beliefs"* and *"valuations."* In people's *"opinions,"* beliefs and valuations are blended in a way that I shall discuss. Though there is not a hard and fast line in people's mental processes between these two types of conception, it is nevertheless useful for our analysis to distinguish between them, as their logical import is different. One of these types of conception is intellectual and cognitive; the other, emotional and volitive.[8] The beliefs express our ideas about how reality actually is, or was, while the valuations express our ideas of how it ought to be, or ought to have been.

A person's beliefs pretend knowledge. As a consequence, it should always be possible to judge the correctness of beliefs by applying the criterion of whether they are true or false and, in the latter case, by gauging the extent and direction in which they deviate from truth. Another dimension is their relative completeness. Here, again, they may be objectively com-

---

8. To stress the subjectivity of the valuation process, I deliberately use the word "valuations" and avoid the term "values" that is so popular in all social science—except in the combination "value premises," where certain valuations have been defined and made explicit for use in research. The common use of the term "values" invites confusion between valuations in the subjective sense, the object of these valuations, and indeed the whole social setting of valuations. The use of the term "values," especially in sociological and anthropological literature, also usually contains a hidden value premise, that a "value" *eo ipse* is valuable in some objective sense; this implies a bias of the *laissez-faire* variety. The term "values" finally gives the association of something solid, homogeneous, and stable while in reality valuations are contradictory and also unstable, particularly in modern society; see the references given in the earlier footnote.

pared with more comprehensive knowledge, and the site of the deficiencies may be determined. A person's valuations, on the other hand—that a social situation is or was "just," "right," "fair," "desirable," or the opposite—cannot be judged and measured by the same objective criteria through comparison with true and fuller knowledge.

When valuations are held by an individual or group, however, they are, like beliefs, a part of reality that can be ascertained by research, though not without difficulty (below, Section 5). One basic difficulty stems from the fact that a person's valuations are usually shifting and contradictory. Behind *behavior* there is not one homogeneous set of valuations but a mesh of struggling inclinations, interests, and ideals. Some of these are held consciously and some are suppressed for long intervals, but all of them work to move behavior in their particular direction.

There are no solid "attitudes," and *behavior normally becomes a moral compromise.* Valuations are, so to speak, located on different levels of the moral personality, in the main corresponding to various degrees of generality of moral judgments.

In our civilization people ordinarily agree that, as an abstract proposition, the more general valuations—felt to be valid in relation to the whole nation or even to all human beings—are morally *"higher"* than those relating to particular individuals or groups. This is not an *a priori* assumption but a generalization founded on empirical observation. We all know that it is so.

In the course of actual day-to-day living, acting, thinking, and talking, a person will be found to focus attention on the valuations on one plane of his moral personality while leaving in the shadows for the time being, the often conflicting valuations on other planes. The basis of this selective focusing is plainly opportunistic.

We are imperfect beings, and it is most often the higher valuations that are pushed into the shadows in everyday living. They are preserved for expression on occasions that are more ceremonial in nature or that in one way or another are isolated from daily life where the *"lower"* valuations more often predominate. Taking a shorter view, these latter valuations are more narrowly selfish, more in the nature of economic, social, or sexual interests and jealousies in a particular setting and at a particular time, and less universally benevolent and humane.

A national trade union convention may, for instance, come out strongly against discrimination against Negroes on the labor market, reflecting valuations on the higher level (below, Section VII). Meanwhile, in a narrow, local setting these higher valuations will be overshadowed by valuations on the lower level—"prejudices," as they are often called when viewed from the higher level—and these lower valuations express themselves in discriminatory practices.

Democracy is "government by means of discussion"; in fact, other forms of government cannot totally or for a long period suppress discussion altogether. Effective political discussion nationally, or internationally, is based on the assumption that there is a wide sharing of common valuations, particularly on the higher level. One group of people or another will be found to invoke and appeal to valuations on that level, thus attempting to reveal and stir up valuation conflicts in other groups.

One difficulty in ascertaining valuations springs from the fact that people often try to conceal them *qua valuations,* particularly the operative ones on the lower level. They try to dress up these valuations as beliefs about reality. People, in their opinions, generally underplay valuations by stating their positions as if they were simply logical inferences from what they believe to be true about reality. They seek the "good reasons" which usually cannot qualify as "true reasons." Their opinions then become what we call *"rationalizations."*

In this process valuations are "objectified" by being presented as beliefs or simple inferences from beliefs— which implies hiding them and thereby also keeping their lack of consistency out of sight. Through this process beliefs become distorted. People succeed in believing what they want to believe, what serves the "purposes" of the underlying valuation compromise. A scientific scrutiny of popular beliefs shows not only that they are often wrong but also that they are twisted in a systematic way. It also shows blind spots of unnecessary ignorance and, on the other hand, an astonishing eagerness to acquire knowledge when it is opportune for the urge to rationalize.

*All ignorance, like all knowledge, tends thus to be opportunist.* Every educational effort aimed at correcting distorted beliefs in a society meets strong resistance. People are interested in hiding their valuations and valuation conflicts or want at least to attempt to preserve an appearance of consistency and order in that sphere. I shall return to this.

# IV · *Illustrations of Opportunistically Distorted Beliefs*

Let me first illustrate what I have said so far, choosing some of my illustrations from a comprehensive study of American civilization observed from the viewpoint of the most unprivileged group, the Negroes. The study was carried out a quarter of a century ago, but the general tendency for beliefs to be distorted in order to rationalize valuations and behavior is as much present now as it was then. Indeed, it operates in all sorts of social relations, in all societies, at all times.

To begin with, the wish to conceal valuations on the lower level was revealed by the white Southerners' reluctance to come out with a straight pronouncement of their personal endorsement of prevailing patterns of segregation and discrimination against Negroes. More often than not, they would project them as other people's valuations, saying that "public opinion" was against a change or that "people down here would not stand for it." Seldom would they come out with a frank statement in the first person that they themselves thought it was right and desirable that these repressive patterns be preserved.

An example of the selective and thereby distorted use of available knowledge is that white Southerners, when brought to consider the extremely low standards of Negro schools, would refer to the relatively small amount Negroes paid in taxes. They inferred from this that what there was of education for the children of the Negroes at that time was heavily subsidized by the white community.[9]

Negroes, on the other hand, were quite commonly equipped with a sophisticated theory that the incidence of indirect taxes on real estate was being transferred to the tenants in the form of higher rents. As a poorer class more frequently living in rented homes, Negroes bore a proportionately heavier burden, so that they paid fully or more than fully for the education of their children.

Likewise, fairly educated whites (including, as I observed at that time, even some doctors of medicine) clung to unsubstantiated and false ideas about the physical characteristics of Negroes—for instance, that

9. A similar thought is prominent today among the white minority in South Africa when they defend their oppressive policy towards the non-white majority there.

they had a peculiar smell, thicker skulls, or larger penises—which Negroes usually did not believe.

Negroes were generally informed of the growing evidence that refined intelligence tests and aptitude tests did not confirm the existence of great inherited differences between whites and Negroes as groups, yet one could find even educated whites who had kept themselves ignorant of it.

As the present time approached and the issue broadened, it was dramatically revealed even to ordinary educated persons that the great majority of Americans—who were living in comfortable circumstances—had acquired a blind spot towards the existence all over America of large enclaves of poverty-stricken and also culturally impoverished people. As I saw it, this was the beginning of a moral and intellectual catharsis, signified and partly caused by an avalanche of statistical studies, books and articles, conferences and speeches. Early in 1964 it led President Lyndon B. Johnson to declare "unconditional war on poverty" and to proclaim the goal of establishing the "Great Society."

This interrelated change of both beliefs and valuations seems later to have been dammed up by the moral, political, and financial effects of the Vietnam war and of the race riots. I do not want to pursue this matter further in this connection. Still, I would suggest that a deeper study of the development of beliefs in different groups and opinion camps during this dramatic period would reveal that, under the pressure of the exploding events on these two fronts in very recent years, changing valuations have been associated with new and gross distortions of beliefs about facts.

The comfortable Americans' traditional ability to live happily on, unconcerned with the numerous and huge poverty pockets in their midst, was developed to the extreme, yet it is nothing unique. A reluctance to learn about the living conditions of the poor is common among the better-off members of Western society.

As a young professor some thirty years ago, I had to examine law students who were requested to have a sprinkling of knowledge about social and economic conditions. More often than today's students, they came from the upper income strata. At that time, half the families in Swedish cities lived in apartments of only two rooms, or less. I used to ask my students what they believed was the size of an average family dwelling. Until they had learned about my interest in that question and had checked up on the facts, their guesses clustered around four or five rooms.

Speaking more generally, the psychological need for rationalization of valuations operating on the lower level gives rise to what I have called "stereotypes" or "popular theories." They are important social facts in every society and can be studied empirically. They consist of complexes of beliefs, twisted to fit the lower-level valuations which they serve to hide or rationalize. In the racial issue referred to above, race by itself is not socially important. It is racial beliefs, expressed as popular theories, that are important.[10] The same is true to a varying degree in other political issues. The valuations which popular theories and stereotypes are meant to conceal or justify give them emotional charge. They are usually uttered with much conviction as if they were statements about facts of extraordinary importance. Under scrutiny, these stereotyped popular theories show up as tangles of grossly false and often contradictory beliefs about reality.

I have chosen my illustrations from internal issues in a nation. Often the beliefs and popular theories in regard to problems of foreign policy, where the facts are more remote from people's ordinary experiences, deviate for this and other reasons even further from rational realism and can easily acquire an almost hysterical load of emotions as support. During the McCarthy-Dulles era the American people recklessly indulged in the veritable nightmare of an imagined Communist world conspiracy against the United States and the entire "free world."

This nightmare—and the completely frantic idea that there was a present danger that the few Communists in this great and powerful country should overthrow constitutional government by violent means—spread and became for a time almost national ideology.

10. *An American Dilemma*, Ch. 4, "Racial Beliefs," pp. 83–112.

It has, for instance, been a main cause of U.S. political and military actions in Vietnam ever since 1949. It affected the intellectual life of nearly the entire nation and left its mark as well on scientific literature and on teaching at all levels. At the same time and to an even greater extent, it was a popular belief among the masses.

In a somewhat toned-down display it covered the whole Western world for a period. After the Second World War the Western countries in Europe depended initially on financial aid from the United States, and their politicians learned quickly that the most effective way to get the United States to be generous in aiding them was to refer to the danger of Communism. Accepting American ideology was thus an opportunistic interest to them. We could also see that when the aid petered out, so did the Europeans' anxiety about the Communist threat.

A Swede has reason to recall from the history of his own country how in the years before the First World War a wave of fear and hatred was worked up against the Russians by conservative forces. All sorts of beliefs were spread about what the Russians at that time did and aimed to do, and these now appear to have been unfounded. Fortunately the wave did not affect the masses of people very deeply. Hjalmar Branting and others on the Left performed a cleansing function which lacked an equivalent in the United States during the later period I mentioned, when most liberals (in confusion and sometimes with twinges of conscience) took refuge in ostentatious anticommunism.[11] But in Sweden at the start of the First World War, it influenced the attitudes in the upper strata decisively in a pro-German direction.

11. *Challenge to Affluence* (New York, Pantheon Books, 1963), Ch. 9, particularly pp. 122 ff.

# V · Suggestions for Opinion Research

Before I leave the problem of the ways in which valuations influence beliefs and mold them in an opportunistic fashion, making them usable for rationalization, I should briefly point out a corollary important for social research.[12]

Reacting to the earlier school of rationalist psychology, we long ago became very impressed by the fact that people do not act and think rationally. Consequently, we established the tradition of *not* bisecting the opinions of people into those components relating to the cognitive aspects of mental processes and those relating to volitional aspects. In opinion poll

12. See *An American Dilemma*, App. 10, pp. 1136–43; (*Value in Social Theory*, Ch. 5, Secs. 4 and 5, pp. 82–88).

questionnaires one can commonly find questions concerning beliefs, concerning almost pure valuations, and concerning opinions in which beliefs and valuations are blended—all these three types usually mixed together without distinction. Yet a clearer differentiation would be of great importance since a study of people's beliefs throws light not only on what they know and do not know but also on the structure of their valuations.

People's beliefs—unlike their valuations—can be directly judged by the objective criteria of correctness and completeness. This fact offers us a clue with which to analyze scientifically the patterns of internally inconsistent and often concealed valuations that exist in the minds of people. The direction and the degree of the deviation of their beliefs from objective, comprehensive knowledge will tell us how people are trying to escape a confrontation of the valuations held on the lower level (implicit in their daily behavior) with the more general valuations which are recognized as morally higher in our society.

From this point of view, it becomes important to chart quantitatively people's knowledge and ignorance on controversial issues. For this purpose certain of the questions in scientific opinion studies should be purged as far as possible of all explicit valuations; they should test only the respondents' conception of a particular part of reality. It should be fairly easy to prepare standard, lucid norms of what represents "objective" knowledge. (In the many problems in which we are ignorant or hesitant, consciousness of our limitations constitutes true knowledge.) For testing beliefs to determine their completeness—and to find the lacunae—some sort of graduated scales should be developed.

The hypothesis is that we almost never face a random lack of knowledge. Ignorance, like knowledge, is purposefully directed. An emotional load of valuation conflicts presses for rationalization, creating blindness at some spots, stimulating an urge for knowledge at others, and, in general, causing conceptions of reality to deviate from truth in determined directions.

If the degree of knowledge and ignorance and also their location and concrete character were analyzed in this way, the valuations and their conflicts could be recorded indirectly but quantitatively—as the heat of distant stars is measured by observing their spectra. The hypothesis behind such research is that ignorance and knowledge are generally not simple and haphazard but are opportunistic. If a major research program were undertaken with this purpose, opinion polls might prove far more valuable than they can be in their present journalistic role.

But, of course, the valuations should also be studied directly insofar as possible. For this purpose other questions should be selected relating to opinions that contain no reference to the more specific reality about which people have beliefs. Valuations are complex and ordinarily conflicting, and an individual focuses attention in his valuation sphere in an opportunist fashion—and his selection and presentation of valuations is probably different in a testing situation from what it is in real life. Hence, indirect analysis of the valuations, through the study of the deviations of beliefs from true and more complete knowledge, is likely to probe more deeply than direct analysis. Normally an individual feels an urge to arrange his valuations so that they may be presented in an orderly and acceptable form. In his beliefs concerning social reality—which are shaped to give the appearance of rational organization to his morals and his behavior—he reveals himself.

When studying valuations by either method—or a combination of them—it is important to observe another distinction: namely that between a person's *"private,"* or "personal," opinion and his *"public,"* or "political," opinion on the same question. These do not necessarily agree; in fact, they seldom agree. Studying this distinction throws light on the dichotomy of (and usually the conflict between) valuations on different levels of generality.

In the Negro problem, for instance, there are often flagrant contradictions between people's valuations about how society ought to be and the valuations implicit in their daily behavior. On the issue of birth control—at least until the recent breakthrough in public opinion—it was easy to prove statistically that a large number of people who publicly condemned birth control and who backed legislative measures to prohibit it must, nevertheless, have practiced it.

# VI · *Valuations Also Depend on Beliefs*

Up to this point we have been discussing ways in which people's beliefs are dependent on their need to rationalize their valuations and, in particular, their need to conceal the conflicts of their valuations. In our rationalist civilization people want to appear consistent in their opinions and want to present reasons for them: hence, they masquerade their valuations as beliefs, which then become distorted. But there is also an influence exerted by beliefs, and particularly by changes in beliefs, upon valuations.

For the most part, people are subjectively honest and seek consistency; openly cynical people are rare if the whole society does not turn cynical. If beliefs are corrected, this exerts pressure on people to change their valuations to such a degree that they can present to themselves and to others what they feel to be consistent opinions, which now must include the corrected beliefs. Normally, such an adjustment should imply a weakening of the valuations on the lower level and a change to greater conformity with those on the higher level.

For this reason a major alteration in the perception of reality very often becomes a combined intellectual and moral catharsis in regard to both beliefs and valuations. We experienced the beginning of such a catharsis in America when the poverty issue was forcibly raised in the last year of the late President John Kennedy, resulting in the pathetic declaration of "unconditional war on poverty" by his successor, President Johnson.

In the Negro problem the correction of some of the derogatory popular beliefs about Negroes—which, as I pointed out, have become stratified in stereotyped and complex popular theories—should gradually and perceptibly change prejudiced opinions harboring valuations and valuation conflicts. When the prejudiced person can retain some of his derogatory beliefs about Negroes only at the price of displaying to others that he is uneducated, he should find it difficult to maintain his prejudiced opinions, including some of his valuations on the lower level.

As earlier false beliefs have served a purpose and satisfied a need, we should not be surprised, however, that their correction meets resistance. People can simply refuse to accept correction and can, at least for a time, stick tenaciously to their false beliefs against evidence. Or they will readjust their stereotyped popular theories so that, in order to rationalize their valuations, they no longer need the support of one or another false belief, which can thus be dropped. In the longer run the effect may be to break down the prejudiced valuations, at least in part.

No really comprehensive, systematic, and conclusive research has ever been done to demonstrate how the rectification of false beliefs—through education and mass information—can influence opinions, the underlying valuations, and the resulting behavior. The effect of television on people's opinion of the Vietnam war might provide a test case. Research on such changes should take into account the time factor, as often it is only over a rather long period that the effect becomes more substantial.

Consideration should also be given to the importance of various formal and informal organizations in our society. Some of them operate to educate the people by trying to get them to accept more correct beliefs and to draw the consequences by scaling down their prejudices. Others, however, particularly on the local level, support resistance to change by providing the individual with assurance that he is not alone in clinging to his old, prejudiced opinions and behavior.

# VII · *The Importance of the State and Other Formal Institutions*

In *An American Dilemma* I had occasion to demonstrate and exemplify that, by the cumulative effects of circular causation, it would be "natural" for race prejudices to spread and grow more intense.[13] I touched then on a special variant of an enigma that has puzzled philosophers for thousands of years: the problem of Good and Evil.

I quoted Thomas Hobbes, who pointed out that the wisest and most virtuous man will hardly leave a print on the sand behind him while an imbecilic crank or criminal can set fire to a whole town. Why, then, is the world not steadily and rapidly deteriorating morally but rather, as we do hope—at least over long periods—progressing?

13. *Op. cit.*, Ch. 3, Sec. 8, pp. 78–80; (*Value in Social Theory*, Ch. 8, Sec. 9, pp. 192–94).

Hobbes raised this question. As we know, his answer was the State, *Leviathan*. Our State is a different one from Hobbes'; it is democratic. Nevertheless, my answer has something basically in common with that of the post-Elizabethan materialist and hedonist.

Of course, the State is collectively made up of and controlled by people, most of them heavily prejudiced, under the influence of competition for jobs and social status, of sex drives, and all sorts of narrow, short-sighted interests, fears, jealousies, and inhibitions that form causative factors of the individuals' behavior and their implicit valuations on the lower level. But when thinking and acting within their formal institutions, particularly the nationwide ones, people more readily permit their higher valuations on the general level to come to consciousness and extend influence.

"The school, in every community, is likely to be a degree more broadminded than local opinion. So is the sermon in church. The national labor assembly is prone to decide slightly above the prejudice of the median member. Legislation will, on the whole, be more equitable than the legislators are themselves as private individuals. When the man in the street acts through his orderly collective bodies, he acts more as an American, as a Christian, and as a humanitarian than if he were acting independently. *He thus shapes social controls which are going to condition even himself.*

"Through these huge institutional structures, a constant pressure is brought to bear on race prejudices, counteracting the 'natural' tendency for it to spread and become more intense. It is the same people who are acting in the institutions and who are manifesting personal prejudices. But they obey different moral valuations on different planes of life. In their institutions they have invested more than their everyday ideas which paralleled their actual behavior. They have placed in them their ideas of how the world rightly ought to be. The ideals thereby gain fortifications of power and influence in society."[14]

This I have characterized as "a theory of social self-healing that applies to the society we call democracy." Besides their direct effects on citizens' behavior, legislation and administration always have the indirect effects of propagandizing for certain ideals. The same is true of decisions, regulations, and declarations of other formal institutions. In adhering to their ideals, institutions have a pertinacity matched only by their considerable flexibility in local and temporary accommodation. In *An American Dilemma* the theory was applied to the American race problem, but it has validity for all problems of social life.

The necessary assumption is, however, that moral cynicism towards the heritage of ideals in our stream of civilization does not come to dominate the institutions of a country as it has done over the race issue in South Africa and as it did over a much broader field in Germany under Nazism. In the United States in recent years the combination of two interrelated

14. *Ibid.*

developments, American warfare in Vietnam and race riots at home, has undoubtedly lowered moral standards in a large part of the population and caused a moral and political isolation of the American government and that part of the American people from almost the whole world. The State has in these cases been instrumental not in raising moral standards but, instead, in lowering them.

# VIII · *The Role of Social Science*

Education sponsored, directed, and financed by the State and other formal institutions may partly and for a time give support to opportunist and false beliefs. This is revealed, for instance, by the recurring criticism and discussion of the content of textbooks. More generally and in the longer view, education is a force correcting these beliefs. Behind education, providing a spur to its long-range trend towards rationalism, is social science.

Like science generally, social science first appeared very early in the history of all civilizations. In the beginning it was deeply embedded in primitive religion and systematized superstitions. But even in very early times, the inclination of students to learn from experience and observation and the considerable flexibility of religious and other doctrines implied advances towards less distorted beliefs.

In the Age of Enlightenment, social science made a gigantic stride towards liberating itself from all influences other than observations of reality and analysis of observations in rational terms. In that glorious era, social science also placed higher valuations closer to the basis of theory. It even tried to "prove" them to be true (Section XVIII below). Although the "proofs" can be shown to be spurious, the very fact that higher valuations were made supreme was an important advance since the responsibility they hold for distorting beliefs is not nearly so great as that of lower valuations.

Since then, progress has been swift and has, on the whole, accelerated. I began this essay by stressing that the ethos of social science is the search for objective truth. This I consider not only a moral precept but also a description of the factual situation. Even if one begins with views distorted opportunistically on a particular problem, the pursuit of social research itself will gradually correct these views. Facts kick, as I sometimes say. In that sense, social science has a demonstrated power of self-healing.

To me, one of the great monuments to the ethos of truth-seeking in social science and to its inherent capacity for leading, in the end, to truer knowledge has been the history of research on inherited group differentials in aptitudes, especially intelligence. The psychologists who more than a half century ago set out to measure innate differences in intelligence between whites and Negroes, men and women, rich and poor, had no doubt that such differences existed and that they were pronounced.

There is truth in the biblical saying that "he that seeketh, findeth"; however, if a scientist seeks what isn't there, he will find it only as long as empirical data are scanty and he allows his logic to be twisted. As the researchers amassed their observations and as they refined their tools for observation and analysis, they found what they had *not* been seeking and what, indeed, was contrary to their preconceptions: the differences disappeared, or at least could not be scientifically established.

Students in the field of social science have imbibed the ethos of truth-seeking so thoroughly that they often appear particularly happy when they arrive at conclusions different from what they had expected or assumed from the start. By increasing true knowledge and purging opportunistic, false beliefs in this way, social science lays the groundwork for an ever more effective education: making people's beliefs more rational, forcing valuations out in the open, and making it more difficult to retain valuations on the lower level opposing those on the higher level.

The great tradition in social science and, particularly, in economics has been for the social scientists to take a direct as well as an indirect responsibility for popular education. There is a recent trend, with which I must register my dissatisfaction, to abandon this great tradition. Through generations even the greatest scholars—and they especially—managed to spare the time from their scientific work to speak to the people in simple terms that laymen could understand. Yet too many social scientists today are increasingly addressing only each other. This trend to false scientism, this forgoing of our responsibility for the formation of public opinion, is apt to decrease the importance of our work for making people more rational.

Another trend works in the same direction. While a great tradition in social science was to express reasoning as clearly and succinctly as possible, the tendency in recent decades has been for social scientists to close themselves off by means of unnecessarily elaborate and strange terminology, often to the point of impairing their ability to understand one another—and perhaps occasionally even themselves.

# IX · *Biases in Research*

The self-healing capacity of social science to which I referred is, however, neither an instantaneous nor a thoroughgoing process. Seldom does it occur easily or completely.

As social scientists we are deceiving ourselves if we naïvely believe that we are not as human as the people around us and that we do not tend to aim opportunistically for conclusions that fit prejudices markedly similar to those of other people in our society. By keeping to higher valuations and by assigning prime importance to observed facts, we only partly purge these biases from our mind.

We are under the influence of tradition in our sciences, of the cultural and political setting of our environment, and of our own peculiar personal makeups. We are not automatons like the electronic machines we use increasingly to master large masses of data.

The result is systematic biases in our work—even in our man-made programming of computing machines— if we do not protect ourselves by means of sociological and psychological insight into the conditions under which we live and work and by means of the logical methods for purging biases (which I will discuss below in Sections XI-XIV). To illustrate my thesis that scientific work is otherwise bound to become biased, I shall refer to some of the fields in which I have had research experience.

The biases are easier to detect and specify when some time has lapsed and some of the conditions have changed. In my book *The Political Element in the Development of Economic Theory,* I analyzed the systematic biases in classical and neoclassical economic theory. The metaphysical moral philosophies of natural law and utilitarianism, from which economic theory once developed, were shown to be an important influence. Within this heritage the fact that economic theory first developed in England (which was then the world's richest country) and that in England the richer strata of society dominated economics (as they did all other forms of higher culture), determined the choice of approaches and of lines of reasoning

(Section XXII below).[15] One example of the biases resulting from this conditioning is, for instance, the fact that the term "unemployment" was not commonly used until late in the nineteenth century[16]—though, of course, unemployment was in fact frequently very high.

When I came to study the controversial Negro problem in America, I found that biases in research were a problem of primary importance.[17] In the extensive discussion of biases in *An American Dilemma,* it is asserted that the scientific literature on the problem was quite generally biased, in different directions and to differing degrees. I found myself quoting authors in order to illustrate opinions about various aspects of the problems more often than to document facts and factual relationships.

In the study of the development problems in South Asia, which has been my latest venture, I have found that all principal concepts, theories, and models have been biased, both in colonial times[18] and after the Second World War.[19] This biased postwar thinking,

15. See also *Rich Lands and Poor*, Pt. II, particularly Ch. 10, pp. 137–49.

16. *Asian Drama,* Vol. 2, Ch. 21, Sec. 8, pp. 984–89.

17. *An American Dilemma,* App. 2, Secs. 1–3, pp. 1035–45; (*Value in Social Theory*, Ch. 7).

18. *Asian Drama,* Ch. 21, Secs. 6–7, pp. 977–84.

19. *Ibid.,* Prologue, Secs. 3–6, pp. 10–24, *et passim* in the several chapters and in the methodological appendices, pp. 1839 ff.

which I have called the "modern approach," is heavily influenced by diplomacy and wishful thinking as manifested in the context of the Cold War. Such systematic biases are facilitated by the uncritical application of scientific approaches worked out for economic analysis in the Western developed countries. Even the commonly used terminology—the "free world," "free Asia," "developing countries," etc.—is systematically biased; these terminological defects indicate the deeper biases in approach.[20]

Biases have freer reign in the studies of South Asia as well as in those of other underdeveloped regions because statistics and other factual information are so scarce and weak. Much of the pretended data, for instance, about "unemployment" and "underemployment," is meaningless or means something entirely different from that which it is assumed to mean, as it has been collected and analyzed by utilizing concepts of the "modern approach" that are inadequate to the realities in these countries so different from the developed countries. Thus the assembling of statistics and other empirical material cannot provide a check on the approach, as a confrontation with facts normally should. The facts do not kick effectively, and the opportunity for the self-healing process, referred to above in Section VIII, is put in abeyance.

The systematic biases operating in research on the

20. *Ibid.*, Prologue, Sec. 3, pp. 10–12, and App. 1, "Diplomacy in Terminology," pp. 1839–42.

development problems in South Asia gain their strength from the fact that the "modern approach" is opportunistic, satisfying the wishes of both radicals and conservatives in the region.[21] It is also opportunistic for people in the rich Western countries. If the "modern approach" were logically tenable and adequate to reality, the underdeveloped countries in South Asia and elsewhere would confront us with much simpler and more manageable policy problems.

Biases lead to a false perception of reality and to faulty policy conclusions. Without further abstract illustration of the prevalence and character of systematic biases in social science, I may only point out that they impair the power of the social sciences to purge distorted and false popular beliefs, which I characterized as the role of these sciences in our society. Since biases in research, like distorted popular beliefs, are opportunistic and, indeed, regularly in line with those beliefs, the biased research may even support them, at least partly and for a time.

The lack of independence of social science research from current beliefs and valuations in the surrounding society is illustrated dramatically by the fact that it rarely blazes the way towards new perspectives. The cue to the continual reorientation of our work has

21. *Ibid.*, Prologue, Sec. 6, pp. 20–24, *et passim* throughout the book.

normally come from the political interests that dominate the society in which we live.[22]

Thus, the deluge of writings on underdeveloped
countries, for instance, reflects the fact that, after the
liberation of these countries from colonial domina-
tion and in the general setting of the Cold War, hap-
penings there have become politically important
in the developed countries as well. The economic and
social conditions in these countries today are not very
different from what they were before the disintegra-
tion of the colonial power system. But at that time the
destiny of these lands and their people was not felt
to be of great political importance in the rich countries.

Likewise, we can be certain that research on the
Negro problem in America in the years to come will
be given a much higher priority by government, foun-
dations, universities, and individual students than it has
been given in the past twenty years, since the Negro
rebellion has now increased the political importance
of such research.

This political conditioning of the *direction* of our
work may simply be a rational way of adjusting it to
the needs felt in the society in which we live and
work. Nonetheless, a social scientist might be excused
for wishing that we, as professionals, had foresight
enough to read the writing on the wall: why should
our societies usually be taken by surprise by events,
be caught unprepared, and forced to improvise?

The fact that social conditioning plays such a

22. *Ibid.,* Prologue, Secs. 2 and 3, pp. 8–12.

decisive role in the choice of field for research should make us more aware and apprehensive of that other type of conditioning: namely, of the *approaches* we choose in research, by which I mean the concepts, models, and theories we use, and the way in which we select and arrange our observations and present the results of our research. That second type of conditioning, though not necessarily the first one, is what leads to biases.

# X · *The Role of Hidden Valuations*

For centuries the tradition in social science has been to conceal the valuations that have determined the scientific approach. Thus, on an elementary level the mechanism of biased research does not differ from the one operating in popular thinking, as I described it in Sections III and IV above. As I noted, social science is never anything other than highly sophisticated common sense.

Like people in general, social scientists are apt to conceal valuations and conflicts between valuations by stating their positions as if they were simply logical inferences from the facts. Since, like ordinary people, they suppress valuations *as valuations* and give only "reasons," their perception of reality easily becomes distorted, that is, biased.

Social scientists want to be objective by "keeping to the facts." It should first be conceded that, by subjecting popular beliefs and scientific assumptions to the test of facts, specific biases have time and again been unmasked. This is what I call the self-healing process in scientific work, which I exemplified in referring to the history of research on intellectual aptitudes of various racial and social groups (Section VIII above).

Nevertheless, biases in social science cannot be erased simply by "keeping to the facts" and refining the methods of dealing with statistical data. Indeed, data and the handling of data are often more susceptible to tendencies towards bias than is "pure thought." The chaos of possible data for research does not organize itself into systematic knowledge by mere observation.

Before there can be a view, a viewpoint must be fixed, and this implies valuation. "Without valuations," wrote my late friend, Louis Wirth, with whom I corresponded on these matters, "we have no interest, or sense of relevance or of significance, and, consequently no object."[23] If, in their attempts to be factual, scientists do not make their viewpoint explicit, they leave room for biases.

Nor can a scientist avoid biases by stopping short of practical or political conclusions. Research

23. In a letter to the author, September 29, 1939.

is no better protected against biases if the scientist refuses to arrange its results into a form suitable for practical and political use.

It is also apparent that, despite assurances to the contrary, practical and political conclusions are almost always drawn nevertheless. Our whole literature is permeated by value judgments, despite prefatory statements to the contrary. But these conclusions are not presented as inferences from explicit value premises; rather, in the age-old fashion, it is claimed they are evident from the nature of things: as part of what is presented as objective data. They are most often introduced by loading the terminology. Words like, for instance, "equilibrium," "balance," "stable," "normal," "adjustment," "lag," or "function" have in all the social sciences served as a bridge between presumably objective analysis and political prescription.[24]

Biases are thus not confined to the practical and political conclusions drawn from research. They are much more deeply seated than that. They are the unfortunate results of concealed valuations that insinuate themselves into research at all stages, from its planning to its final presentation. As a result of their concealment, they are not properly sorted out and can thus be kept undefined and vague.

The underlying psychology of bias is simple. Every student, as a private person and as a responsible

24. *An American Dilemma,* pp. 1047 ff.

citizen, is more or less entangled in the web of conflicting valuations that I discussed in Section III. Like the layman, the scientist is influenced by the psychological need for rationalizations.

The same is true of every executive responsible for other people's research and of the popular and scientific public before which the scientist performs—and whose reactions he has opportunistic reasons to respect. The fact that his fellow scientists usually are conditioned in the same way strengthens the effect of the irrational influences. Generally speaking, we can observe that the scientists in any particular institutional and political setting move as a flock, reserving their controversies and particular originalities for matters that do not call into question the fundamental system of biases they share.

Opposing the most honest determination on the part of all concerned and, primarily, on the part of scientists themselves to be open-minded, the common need for rationalization will tend in this way to influence the concepts, models, and theories applied; hence it will also affect the selection of relevant data, the recording of observations, the theoretical and practical inferences drawn explicitly or implicitly, and the manner of presentation of the results of research. For all these operations taken together, I use the term "approach."

The method of detecting biases is simple although somewhat laborious. When the unstated value premises of research are kept hidden and for the most part vague, the results presented contain logical flaws. When inferences are confronted with premises, there is found to be a *non sequitur* concealed, leaving the reasoning open to invasion by uncontrolled influences from the valuation sphere. This element of inconclusiveness can be established by critical analysis. My book *The Political Element in the Development of Economic Theory* was mainly concerned with such a critical analysis, demonstrating logical flaws of economic theory.

# XI · *Bringing the Valuations Out in the Open*

At this point of the argument it should be stated most emphatically that the fault in most contemporary as well as earlier social science research is not in its lack of "objectivity" in the conventional sense of independence from all valuations. On the contrary, every study of a social problem, however limited in scope, is and must be determined by valuations. A "disinterested" social science has never existed and, for logical reasons, can never exist.

However, the value premises that actually and of necessity determine social science research are generally hidden. The student can even remain unaware of them. They are then left implicit and vague, leaving the door open to biases.

The only way in which we can strive for "objectivity" in theoretical analysis is to expose the valuations to full light, make them conscious, specific, and explicit, and permit them to determine the theoretical research. In the practical phases of a study, the stated value premises, together with the data (established by theoretical analysis with the use of the same value premises) should then form the premises for all policy conclusions.

I am arguing here that value premises should be made explicit so that research can aspire to be "objective"—in the only sense this term can have in the social sciences. But we also need to specify them for the broader purposes of honesty, clarity, and conclusiveness in scientific inquiry.

# XII · *Terminological Escapism*

This is the appropriate place to insert a brief note on the systematic efforts made in conventional social science to avoid value-loaded terms and to substitute for them terms without palpable associations to valuations. Since by logical necessity valuations permeate all research from beginning to end, these efforts can be shown to have been in vain and, indeed, to have added to the confusion of thought inherent in all attempts to carry on research without value premises.

Far into the nineteenth century and even later, social scientists still believed that there were valuations that could be objectively ascertained to be true and were thus similar to other conceptions of reality that could be true or false(Sections XVII and XVIII below). The fact that our knowledge of these allegedly "true valuations" was still imperfect, particularly in regard to their measurability, did not impair their existence as part of reality. Writing as late as in the beginning of this century, Knut Wicksell, a most distinguished economist in the hedonist and utilitarian tradition, reflected:

"Perhaps someday the physiologists will succeed in isolating and evaluating the various human needs for bodily warmth, nourishment, variety, recreation, stimulation, ornament, harmony, etc., and thereby lay a rational foundation for the theory of consumption."

Even if social scientists of later generations have seldom disclosed their faith as bluntly as Wicksell, they have continued to work on the assumption that there are objective valuations which in principle could be known, even if there are difficulties in ascertaining them. From an early date—indeed, since the time of Bentham—there has been, however, a clear tendency to hide these valuations by means of innocent-sounding terminology.

In economic theory the retreat from hedonist psychology, which in turn was the cornerstone of utilitarian moral philosophy, was demarcated by the Italian sociologist and economist Vilfredo Pareto in his coining the term "*ophilimité*" as a substitute for "utility." There has been a continuous proliferation of terminological innovations of that kind. The whole of modern welfare theory, on which so much intelligence has been wasted in recent years, is saturated with that type of escapism. It is a body of theory which would contain nothing if it did not implicitly incorporate one version or another of the old, discredited rationalistic psychology and utilitarian moral philosophy. By implying them—as the practical conclusions make evident that it does—it becomes unfounded and false.[25]

The employment of algebraic formulas (however useful they may be for mastering complicated relationships), of Greek letters, and of other symbols facilitates the escape from stating clearly implied assumptions nd, in particular, from being aware of the valuation load of main concepts.

In the other social sciences as well, much of the very considerable attention devoted in recent decades to exuberant terminology is of the same character. It is to a great degree an elaborate attempt to "objectify" what is not, and cannot be, simply objective.

In studies of a more specific and practical character, however, there are fewer such attempts, as I might illustrate from the area of the Negro in America.[26]

"The scientific work on the Negro in politics has been centered upon disfranchisement. This means that the interest has been defined out of the notion that the extraordinary thing to be studied is the fact that often in America the Negro is not given the right to suffrage as other citizens. In the same vein the work on the

25. *The Political Element in the Development of Economic Theory*, Ch. 4, pp. 80–103, and Appendix by Paul Streeten, pp. 208–17.
26. *An American Dilemma*, App. 2, Sec. 6, p. 1063; (*Value in Social Theory*, Ch. 7, Sec. 4, pp. 162–63.)

Negro's legal status has been focused upon the specific disabilities of the Negro under the law. Negro education has likewise been studied under the main viewpoint of discrimination. The same is true of the research on the Negro as a breadwinner. Negro standards of living have been compared with those of whites. The Negro's share in social welfare policy has been measured by the standards of equality."

Discrimination, which is of course a heavily value-loaded term, has thus been the key word for most studies of the Negro problem in the United States. This term—and all its synonyms and specifications—and also the entire approach to the Negro problem, which it signifies, were obviously derived out of the precepts of the American Creed. By this expression I mean the particularly explicit system of valuations on the higher level that has been constantly declared and kept explicit in public discussion in the United States and is contained in the Constitution and many other national institutions and which, I believe, in spite of serious setbacks, represents the historical trend.

Even in the Negro problem, there have occasionally been attempts by particular authors to introduce new and less colorful words in order to be more "objective." But they have never had much effect and, because of this, have been fairly harmless.[27] As a rule the new words have meant the same thing, and then the

27. See my essay " 'Value-loaded' Concepts" in *Money, Growth, and Methodology and Other Essays in Economics in Honor of Johan Akerman,* Hugo Hegeland, ed. (Lund, C W K Gleerups Bokförlag, 1961), pp. 273–88.

only result has been to conceal from awareness the implied valuations.

In a country like the United States—however much these higher valuations are disregarded in daily life—the important thing is that exceptions are acknowledged as wrong from the point of view of the national ethos. In *An American Dilemma* the systematized valuations entailed in the American Creed were given the role of explicit value premises and specified for the various problems.[28]

In the study of underdeveloped countries the drive to "objectify" research is apparent, for instance, in the common attempts to give a definition of development—and underdevelopment—without relying on value premises. This is, of course, not possible. It leads to gross arbitrariness. In *Asian Drama* a whole chapter was devoted to making explicit the value premises applied in that study and to explaining my motives for choosing them.[29]

In brief, what has been said in this section is that there is nothing wrong, *per se*, with value-loaded concepts if they are clearly defined in terms of explicitly stated value premises. If they are not so defined but the implied valuation is concealed, they are certainly providing entrance to biases. If this occurs, it is then not

28. *Op. cit.*, Introduction and Ch. 2, pp. xli–lv and 26–49 *et passim;* (*Value in Social Theory*, Ch. 4, pp. 65–67).
29. *Op. cit.*, Ch. 2, pp. 49–69, cf. Prologue, Sec. 9, pp. 31–34, and Apps. 1, 1839–42, and 2, Pts. II–IV, pp. 1859–1940.

the result of their load of valuations but of their concealment of them; the valuations can then be kept vague. Inventing new terms is no way out. They can only serve to
give us a false sense of security and to deceive the general public. If the new terms represent the same approach
to the reality to be studied as the old, familiar, value-
loaded terms, there has been no change, and they will
soon become equally value-loaded.

# XIII · *The Choice of*
# *Value Premises*

Value premises in social science research must satisfy a number of conditions.[30]

They must be *explicitly stated* and not concealed as implied assumptions. They should be as *specific* and *concrete* as the valuation of reality requires in terms of factual knowledge. They must be *purposefully selected* as they are *not, a priori,* self-evident or generally valid on the grounds of being founded only on facts or on the "nature of things." They are thus a *volitional* element in research, needed there as in all purposive activity. They have therefore only a *hypothetical* character inasmuch as it is possible for

30. See *An American Dilemma*, App. 2, Sec. 4, pp. 1057–64, (*Value in Social Theory*, Ch. 7, Sec. 4, pp. 153–64); and *Asian Drama*, Ch. 2, pp. 49–69.

the inclination of will to differ. Certain epistemological difficulties related to this last requirement and some others mentioned below will be discussed in the next section.

If rationality is one of the value premises, as is normally the case in our type of civilization, the set of premises must not include mutually incompatible value premises but must form a *consistent* system.

The last requirement, in particular, and also some of those mentioned in the following section, imply that the value premises *cannot be entirely* a priori, *independent* of research. Research should start by giving attention to some value premises which it would seem appropriate to utilize, but it must be prepared to adjust these continually.

Value premises must be applied not only to *ends* but also to *means*. The thesis of utilitarianism—that nothing is good or bad in itself but only because of its good or bad results—is not realistic since people actually evaluate means, too. The same is true in relation to *side effects* of the achievement of a certain end by certain means.[31]

31. "Das Zweck-Mittel-Denken in der Nationalökonomie," *Zeitschrift für Nationalökonomie*, Vol. IV, No. 3 (1933); (*Value in Social Theory*, Ch. 10, pp. 206–30).

# XIV · *Difficulties and the Ways to Overcome Them*

The value premises should not be chosen arbitrarily. They must be founded on people's actual valuations. This requirement for *"realism"* in a specific sense of the term cannot be disregarded. It represents, however, the main reason for difficulties.

We may start our discussion by considering what "realism" in this sense would imply *prima facie*. The principle of selection of value premises should be their *relevance,* determined by the actual valuations of persons and groups in society. Within the circle of relevance so determined there is an even smaller circle of *significance,* taken to denote valuations held by substantial groups of people or by small groups with substantial power.[32]

32. I have here assumed that relevance and significance should be determined in relation to the society under study. A society can, however, be studied from the viewpoint of relevant and significant valuations in another society; see *Asian Drama,* Ch. 2, Sec. 1, p. 50.

The realization of the value premises must, moreover, be *feasible*. Valuations which aim for the impossible, of course, should not be chosen as value premises for research but should be criticized theoretically as infeasible after a study of the facts. This is another example in which the value premises are not *a priori* independent of research. This theoretical criticism in terms of feasibility is, indeed, one of the most important tasks of social science.

The *scientific basis* for ascertaining the valuations in society is poor. Existing opinion studies do not meet our requirements (Section V above). For the time being the social scientist is generally forced to resort to impressionistic observations and to speculation.

Whatever method is applied to expose people's real valuations, the fact that valuations are bound up with beliefs will present a primary difficulty. Beliefs influence valuations just as valuations influence beliefs (Section VI above). To a scientist engaged in making society more rational, it must be questioned whether he should not want to use the valuations people *would have* if their beliefs were *correct* and not distorted. For this reason alone, the determination of the valuations would become an even more difficult task.

Moreover, valuations to be used as value premises should most often refer to a *future* situation. Particularly in broader issues, this situation may be far off. It might represent the results of great changes on all sorts of levels and even in the institutional structure of society. To draw inferences about people's valuations in radically changed circumstances in the future is hazardous even if present valuations have been ascertained.

A fourth and fundamental difficulty springs from the fact that valuations are *conflicting*. Conflicts rage not only between individuals and groups but also within individuals. People do not have uncomplicated, homogeneous, and consistent valuations; they live in moral conflicts and compromises. This makes both the observation of valuations and the imputation of power to various valuations a most delicate problem. The compromise may change in time and fluctuate according to circumstances.

However, one consideration indicates that these last difficulties—the relation of valuations to more correct beliefs, the long-term validity of valuations in the future, and the allowance for valuation conflicts— ought not be insurmountable.

It is the rationalizations of valuations on what we have called the lower level that lead to distorted beliefs. The requirement that value premises correspond to valuations as they would be when beliefs are corrected will generally imply that the *valuations on a higher level* should be utilized. Broadly, the effect of the requirement that the value premises should be valid for a long future period is the same. And the importance given to the valuations on the higher level, motivated by these two requirements, should to a large extent dissolve the valuation conflicts by pushing aside the valuations on the lower level that regularly conflict with those on the higher one.

As I have pointed out, in day-to-day living the valuations on the higher level are for opportunistic reasons largely concealed; nonetheless, they are ordinarily given a *very explicit expression* by the State and by the several formal institutions within the State and can easily be established by observation. They are usually fairly homogeneous, without inner conflicts (see below, however).

I gave as an example the American Creed, which I specified for use as value premises in *An American Dilemma* (Section XII above).

In *Asian Drama* I pointed out that the Modernization Ideals in the countries of South Asia are now likewise forming a sort of national ethos, expressed as motivation for all planning and all public policies.[33] They form what is nearly the ideological framework for every major policy discussion in these countries.

At the same time that study leads to the general conclusion that, with the actual and foreseeable population increase and other facts and trends in the region, a considerable modernization in terms of these ideals will be necessary in order to prevent a catastrophic development. They cannot return to traditional society or even leave society as traditional as it still is. In that respect these countries have now passed "the point of no return." This adds to the reasons for choosing

33. *Ibid.*, Ch. 2, Secs. 2 and 3, pp. 51–57.

the Modernization Ideals as the value premises for study, although they might conflict with popular feelings among many groups of people.

If thus the value premises were chosen from the valuations on the higher level, the requirement of realism in terms of relevance, significance, and feasibility from which I started would be *converted* into a new requirement: the necessity of *asserting by empirical research* the whole range of operative valuations, including those on the lower level, the emerging valuation conflicts, and their consequences in distorted beliefs. All these things become important in the theoretical study of conditions and their development when this study is carried out with the higher valuations serving as value premises.

In contemporary society there is a great distance between actual facts and the realization of value premises when valuations on the higher level are used as value premises. Of course, this is particularly true in underdeveloped countries, but not only there is it true. The value premises then imply that a development *in the direction of their realization* is accepted as desirable, however far the society under study might be from this actual realization.

In a particular case the study might reveal that a society cannot be expected to move in the desired direction at all but may actually be moving in the opposite direction. This, by itself, does not impair the logic of studying that society by using those value premises. The practical conclusions from such a study would stress the needs for increasing efforts to give more significance to the value premises.

Even if the valuation conflicts are principally between valuations on the higher level, on the one hand, and those on the lower level, on the other, there may be and obviously often are conflicts between valuations on the higher level as well. It can be assumed that in our rapidly changing society this type of valuation conflict may be increasing in importance.

Ideally, therefore, a study should use *several alternative* sets of value premises. This last requirement can for *practical reasons* be met only very partially. We should not forget that the value premises determine the whole approach to a problem and have relevance for the definition of concepts, the formulation of theory, and the methods of observations and of presenting results. To work with several approaches *at the same time* would ordinarily tax our research resources beyond their capacity.

In order not to complicate the work excessively, then, one solution is to select *a single set* of value premises. This set can be called *instrumental*, and it can be stressed that other significant sets of value premises can be introduced at a later stage of the study to make judgments possible in terms of alternative valuations.

But we must not deceive ourselves on this point:

the selection of the instrumental norm has *material significance*. The whole approach in theoretical research becomes determined by this norm. We have thus given the particular set of value premises selected as instrumental a *strategically favorable* position in the study.

It is not a bias, for the approach to research has been determined under conscious control and with the aid of explicit valuations. This closes the door to arbitrariness, as it is the implicit but hidden valuations that lead to the inconclusiveness in conventional research, making biases possible. Yet measured by the standards of what would be ideal and considering the possible existence of other sets of value premises, this is one-sided, and the student should be aware of this.

When all this is said, the method of working with one single set of explicit value premises, however selected, is nevertheless vastly superior to the naïve traditional approach of tucking the valuations under the carpet. By spelling out the value premises actually utilized, reasoning becomes clarified.

Even if in a particular study these value premises have been reached and specified to an extent by impressions and conjectural reasoning and are less concrete and precise than is desirable, attention is given to the role that valuations have played in the study and to their importance for both the theoretical and practical research performed. Anyone wishing to challenge the choice of value premises is then, at least, relieved of the cumbersome task of discovering through immanent criticism the implied valuations and the ways in which they have determined the approach and the results.

Finally, it should overcome the inhibitions against drawing practical and political conclusions openly, systematically, and logically. This method would consequently render social research a much more powerful instrument for guiding rational policy formation.

I am not pretending to have arrived at a final and fully satisfactory solution of the methodological problem raised in this essay. But I do insist that if we place ourselves under the obligation to spell out, in as definite terms as possible, a set of instrumental value premises—however they have been reached and whichever they may be—and if we allow them to determine our approach, the definitions of our concepts, and the formulation of our theories, this represents an advance towards the goals of honesty, clarity, and effectiveness in research. These are steps in the direction of "objectivity" in the only sense this concept can be understood.

# XV · *No Moral Nihilism*

The preceding presentation of the problem of valuations and their role in social science is founded upon the recognition that valuations, unlike beliefs, cannot be judged by the criteria of truth and completeness. Valuations are subjective facts.

This implies what is sometimes called "value relativism." The acceptance of this basic assumption should not be thought, however, to constitute an inhibition or obstacle to arguing a moral point of view.

On the contrary, by insisting on the necessity of value premises in all research, the social sciences should be opened more effectively to moral criticism. It would then be impossible to classify economics as a "dismal science" in the sense of its being closed to moral considerations. Economists working in the conventional mode, attempting to conceal valuations basic to their research, can, however, often be rightly censured in this way, and on logical grounds.

Indeed, no social science or particular branch of social research can pretend to be "amoral" or "apolitical." No social science can ever be "neutral" or simply "factual," indeed not "objective" in the traditional meaning of these terms. Research is always and by logical necessity based on moral and political valuations, and the researcher should be obliged to account for them explicitly.

When these valuations have been brought out into the open, anyone who finds a particular piece of research to have been founded on what he considers wrong valuations can challenge it on that ground. He is also invited to remake the study and remodel its findings by substituting another, different set of value premises for the one utilized. Indeed, argumentation in moral and political terms will be stimulated and greatly facilitated when conventional social science is robbed of its false claims of being able to ascertain relevant and significant facts and even reach practical conclusions without explicit value premises.

Value relativism is thus very emphatically *not moral nihilism*. In our souls we all harbor complex systems of valuations on different levels of our moral personality. Our daily life is a continuous string of moral compromises between valuations on a higher and a lower level. We all have the opportunity to strive to give more power to the valuations on a higher level—in our own life and in the life of our community and of our nation. We can even reach out and appeal in these terms to foreign governments and to their people. The scientific study of society should increase, not decrease, the effectiveness of moral and political discussion.

Social science has always based its work on the morals of the valuations on the higher level (see Section XVII below), in this respect following the similar tendency of the people at large when they are acting in formal institutions (Sections VII above). As we also observed (Section VIII above), this is one of the explanations for the fact that social research has not been entirely ineffective in rectifying people's distorted beliefs, as their distortion is usually caused by opportunistic attempts to conceal valuations on the lower level and their conflict with those on the higher level. To some extent, social research has even been successful in purging valuations on the lower level by correcting distorted beliefs.

Undoubtedly, however, the traditional and still conventional tendency in social research to be "pseudo-objective" and to conceal the value premises implicit in a particular approach has weakened it as an intellectual and moral force in our society. By having to come out in the open with its basic valuations, social research will become more effective in serving the purpose of intellectual and moral catharsis—which is our hope for the improvement of society.

# XVI · *The Respect for Life*

And there this essay could end. But I should
like also to discuss a matter somewhat outside my main
concern about the way in which we are conditioned
as social scientists when we do research and about
the logical means at our disposal for avoiding biases;
I should like to consider the fact that there seem to
exist certain moral principles on the "highest" level
of generality that are common for different historical
epochs and even for different civilizations.

From a methodological point of view, the question
arises whether these seemingly immutable moral principles could be applied as supreme value premises
relieving us of the duty of entering deeper into the
complex reality of people's actual valuations. Do they
break with the "valuation relativism" upon which my

analysis has been founded? Do they provide a logical shortcut that makes it unnecessary to study the actual valuations in society, their conflicts, and the distorted beliefs?

One such supreme moral principle, which in its abstract formulation seems to have unanimous support everywhere and at all times, is, for instance, the respect for human life. An early formulation was the Hippocratic oath, which has in substance remained the recognized ethos of medical men in all countries.

In reality this principle is complicated by certain moral dilemmas: mercy killing, for instance, or conflicts of interest arising from the transplantation of human organs or, more generally, the financial and fiscal costs involved in curing ills and preventing deaths that even in the richest countries could take an unlimited part of the national income. Yet these complications and the fact that they upset us only testify to the existence and influence of the basic moral principle, even though difficulties are encountered in its practical application.

The vitality of the principle shows up in the policy problem created by the recent population explosion in the underdeveloped countries.[34] Generally speaking, it has been accepted as a moral imperative that the efforts in these countries to improve the health situation and bring down death rates—which are the direct cause of the population explosion—must continue and

34. *Ibid.*, Ch. 27, Sec. 9, 1430–35.

that the only feasible remedy must be to attempt to bring down the birth rates as well.

Occasionally, if rather seldom, doubts are expressed about the rationality of the efforts to save lives in the underdeveloped countries. However, these are more often expressed in the rich countries than in the underdeveloped countries themselves.[35] Otherwise the principle seems to have a very high relevance and significance in our society, and the ensuing population policy promoting birth control cannot offhand be deemed infeasible.

A more common and serious lapse from this moral principle is the almost general acceptance to date of war as a possible means of national policy. Moreover, the rules of international law aimed at protecting the civilian population have in recent decades been allowed to disintegrate.[36] The two superpowers and other states as well are now equipping themselves at rising and, indeed, fantastic financial costs for mass murder on an equally fantastic scale.

Even without the use of the most murderous of the new weaponry, wars in recent times have claimed civilian lives increasingly, often with a concentration on poor people and without sparing women and chil-

35. *Ibid.*
36. E.L.M. Burns, *Megamurder* (New York, Pantheon Books, 1967).

dren. The conduct of the Vietnam war represents the current culmination of this sinister trend.

The fact that this war is being discussed as a moral problem in the whole world and even in the United States can from one point of view be seen as a confirmation of the tenacity of the moral principle that human life should be respected. From another point of view, however, the relative weakness of such a moral reaction—particularly in the United States, whose involvement in the war has been permitted to escalate with increasing cruelty—testifies to the low relevance and significance of the principle as a valuation of importance for actual policy.

Other such testimonies are the refusal of the United States Senate to ratify the Geneva Protocol of 1925 against the use of certain particularly cruel means of warfare and, even more important, the fact that this has not created any public uproar in the United States, even among its intellectual and moral elite. Not even the powerful church organizations have protested effectively.

In the competitive situation created by modern military technology it is difficult to see how the application as a value premise of the moral principle discussed in this section could logically lead to any other practical conclusion than *radical pacifism.* No other competing valuation would seem capable of pro-

ducing an acceptable compromise. The heroic excla-
mation "Give me liberty or give me death" does not
fit a situation in which war preparations are made to
kill tens of millions of people, of whom the great
majority cannot be assumed to participate in that
heroism and, in any case, have no say in choosing it.

Pacifism has, however, little popular appeal in any
country. Political efforts are directed at the humbler
goal of reaching intergovernmental agreements on
disarmament or rather on some regulation or possibly
restriction of the armament race. While there are no
real pressures from a popular movement to achieve
such agreements, there are, on the contrary, widespread
nationalistic suspicions, particularly though not exclusively in the United States and the Soviet Union, supported by strong vested interests in the "military-
industrial complex." And even these limited efforts at
disarmament have so far been largely unsuccessful.

The moral principle of respect for human life, commonly recognized as supreme, clearly has little significance as a valuation that is operative in the formation
of national policies. Furthermore, actual world development does not tend to strengthen people's support
for this moral principle. Naturally, this does not imply
that it should not qualify as the value premise for
research on war and peace. But research efforts must
then be directed upon observing and analyzing popular valuations, valuation conflicts, and distorted
beliefs responsible for this unfortunate development.

When it comes to scientific research—theoretical or practical—a person who, for instance, as a part of his religious faith, believes in absolute moral principles is not in a situation different from those of other researchers.

# XVII · *The Egalitarian Principle*

Before I end, I want in this and the following sections to touch briefly on one more general moral principle: namely, the principle that all human beings have equal rights and that equalization of their living and working conditions is a supreme ideal. This principle is of special interest in the present context as it has been placed at the very basis of modern economic and social theory.

But it goes as far back in mankind's history as we can discern. All great religions (including even Hinduism, on a higher level) and related moral philosophies have been egalitarian.[37] Most certainly this is true of Christianity.

It is still a largely unsolved historical and sociolog-

37. *Asian Drama*, Ch. 3, Sec. 2, pp. 74–81, *et passim.*

ical problem why and how this shining vision of the dignity of the individual human being and of his basic right to equal opportunity originated so early and so generally in different civilizations, and how it maintained itself on the level of a supreme ideal through untold centuries of blatant inequality and oppression. Another unsolved problem is whether and to what extent in different regions and in different periods the ideal nevertheless helped modify public policies and private behavior a bit more in the favor of the poor.

In a general sense we know that the more recent systematic social reforms in the interest of the poor have seldom or never emanated from religion and have rather been associated with secularization. Religion's role has been permissive at most; *ex post,* it has offered its blessing for what has already happened or is happening under other influences.[38]

Mohandas Gandhi was almost the first in South Asia in modern times to raise the equality issue forcefully, yet this hardly constitutes an exception, for he acted as a post-Victorian liberal in the English tradition. The religion from which he could claim support was not the popular religion existing all around him: that served mainly as a fortification for the harshly inegalitarian social and economic stratification of the largely stagnant Indian society.[39] Gandhi had to appeal to religion on a higher level as preserved in

38. *Ibid.,* Ch. 16, Sec. 4–5, pp. 749–56, *et passim.*
39. *Ibid.,* Ch. 3, Sec. 7, pp. 103–12.

sacred documents and unworldly, stereotyped formulas scarcely comprehensible on a popular level.

It was the genius of Gandhi to translate these formulas into the religious folklore of his country, mixing them with ingredients from other religions and from humanitarian thoughts in secular literature everywhere and joining it all together with the nationalistic quest for liberation from British rule. In this manner he reached a sort of popular adherence to the egalitarian principle. It was merely partial, however, and greatly confused. Certain exceptions were to be found among the Westernized upper strata, who—in the tradition of secular English liberal thought—readily understood the principle, although their self-interests and the established system of attitudes and institutions in Indian society did not permit many of them to act accordingly.

# XVIII · *The "Proofs" of the Principle*

The modern social sciences were born in the Age of Enlightenment, which was certainly the great ebullition of pent-up secularization. An ultra-radical version of the doctrine of equality was then sharpened into a particularly clear and cutting theoretical instrument of "objective" valuation. It was "proved." And it was placed at the very roots of social and particularly economic theory and in this way fastened at the rock bottom of Western (and, of course, later Communist) speculation.[40]

From the philosophy of natural law emerged the

40. The text here and in the following sections gives only an extremely condensed recapitulation of some main sections in *Rich Lands and Poor*, Pt. II, pp. 109–68, and *The Political Element in the Development of Economic Theory*, Chs. 2–7, pp. 23–190; see also *Value in Social Theory*, Ch. 2, pp. 9–64.

doctrine of labor's moral superiority as title to property: labor was the only "creator of wealth." It materialized in the classical (and later Marxian) theory of "real value," which assumed labor to be the only "factor of production."

From natural law came also the idea that "all men are born equal." This doctrine was understood primarily in the moral sense that all have the same rights in society. It would hold true even if natural endowments were not equal. The fact that a man was less gifted should not infringe upon his rights. Of course, the moralistic equality doctrine was strengthened by the tendency in the philosophy of natural law since the time of Locke towards a naturalistic doctrine as well, minimizing individual or at least group differentials in regard to inborn capacities and aptitudes.

The olden concept of "general welfare" was elaborated in utilitarian moral philosophy and clearly perceived as the maximization in society of the net value of "pleasures" and "pains." The undisputed assumption that in the social calculus every human being should be counted as equal to every other and the almost equally old idea of the diminishing "marginal utility" of an income, provided "proof" for the principle that equalization of wealth and income was in the interest of society.

In this way the principle of equality was established as a logical inference from alleged premises of facts or Laws of Nature. When critically scrutinized, however, these "proofs" turn out to be empty meta-

physics with no relation to reality. It remains important even today to demonstrate this in some detail.
Despite much terminological escapism, conventional
economic theory remains, as I have pointed out, largely
in the molds provided long ago by psychological hedonism and the moral philosophies of natural law and
utilitarianism.

In fact, economic theory along the classical and
neoclassical line became the most elaborate formulation of that psychology and these moral philosophies.
The symbiosis was so close that several of the most
prominent economists in this line were, at the same
time, the leading psychologists and moral philosophers—until that later epoch when the economists
began trying to escape into innocent-sounding terminology in order to establish a realm of "pure economics"
(Section XII above). This happened at about the
same time that the study of psychology turned away
from hedonism.

The failure of the "proofs" of the egalitarian principle to stand up to logical criticism do not impair
it as valuation. If a valuation cannot be "proved" to
be true, neither can it be "proved" to be untrue. It
can simply exist as a fact. As a valuation, the principle
may have the full support of our sentiments inasmuch
as it corresponds to our concept of the way things
ought to be in our society and the world.

Its universality and timelessness rather implies that,
on the highest level of our valuation sphere, it is, in
fact, a moral ambition of all mankind. It is a living

ideal and, as such, part of social reality: a valuation actually perceived by people to be morally right. In the world as it is, however, we should not except it to determine our private behavior or public policies to a very great degree.

# XIX · *Nature and Nurture*

Before further discussion of the dichotomy between radical egalitarianism in principle and conservative acceptance of a very inegalitarian society in practice, I should touch upon a related problem of cardinal importance for social reform: namely, the relative importance of nature and nurture.

Rudolf Kjellén, a brilliant Swedish political scientist active at the turn of the century and during its first few decades, once ventured the observation that a radical person is inclined to believe that the occasion makes the thief while the conservative is apt to suspect that the thief is likely to find the occasion.

According to radicals, the blame and responsibility for what is imperfect in society rests with the environment which can be changed. The individual and, thereby, society can be improved by interference in the conditions of his life.

The conservatives, on the contrary, think that it is human nature and not environment which, on the whole, makes individuals and society what they are. Human nature is unchangeable. This is a reason and a justification for the conservatives' scepticism in regard to social reform and public interferences generally to improve social conditions. They are therefore inclined towards a policy of *laissez-faire*, or do-nothing.

As I mentioned, the moral philosophies of the Enlightenment, which formed the basis for economic and social theory, tended to depreciate differences in human nature, at least between groups. Man and society could be reformed by altering social institutions. This implied an environmental and interventionist approach to social problems. Again religion, and in this case particularly Christianity, had broadly anticipated this radical approach both by presenting the possibility of conversion and a change of heart on the part of the individual and by stressing that faith should result in good deeds which usually implied that they would have good effects.

Returning to the moral philosophies of the Enlightenment, however, it should be noted that one set of inferences from their secularist rationalism gave food for conservatism and worked against the basic environmental approach. By ranking *homo sapien* as an animal in the natural order it gave emphasis to human nature. It made it easier at the same time to assume on *a priori* grounds that there could be distinct species of men, with differing endowments, just as there are species of monkeys and dogs.

It was thus in the eighteenth century that the word and concept "race" was born—I have described the racial doctrine as an illegitimate child of the Enlightenment. For example, it raised the possibility of rationalizing Negro slavery by arguments of racial inferiority instead of by the earlier theological justification that the Negroes were imported pagans. Later, Darwin's theory of the survival of the fittest could be used for explaining innate qualitative differences between social and economic classes as a result of evolution, which then was assumed to be desirable *per se*.

During the nineteenth century this idea—which was so contrary to the Enlightenment philosophers' depreciation of inborn differences between groups of people and to their environmental approach to social and economic problems—rather tended to gain ground. In Section VIII I mentioned that the psychologists who around the turn of the century began to measure the difference in intelligence and other aptitudes between whites and Negroes—and between men and women and rich and poor—did not doubt that there were differences and that they were substantial.

Under closer study this hypothesis was not proved. At the same time the anthropologists came to deprecate the idea that the major groupings of mankind represented different species of human beings. Modern research has generally tended to confirm the basic beliefs of the Enlightenment philosophers. The contrary beliefs—that there are dissimilar groups of people in our society—however, remained very much alive in the convictions of laymen—and often in those of philosophers and theorists as well, particularly when they were somewhat removed from their doctoral pursuits.

The relative importance of nature and nurture is a question of facts, and beliefs can be proved to be true or false by research. Though beliefs in regard to these problems are not valuations, I have touched on the matter because it is of fundamental importance to the environmental approach, without which the egalitarian principle loses much of its practical sense.

# XX · *Paradoxes*

Aspects of the doctrinal development I am sketching here are paradoxical. In the period around the end of the eighteenth and the beginning of the nineteenth century, when the egalitarian principle was enunciated most explicitly and given particular emphasis in the advanced Western countries and when its "proofs" were vindicated most courageously, the economic and social inequalities between regions, social classes, and individuals in those countries were appalling, compared with the much greater equality that has since been accomplished. How could the egalitarian principle blossom so freely at just that time?

Very little was done during that period in the way of reform policies designed to mitigate existing inequalities. Why was the principle so inconsequential for public policy? At this time, it is true, there were already radicals who took the principle seriously and who projected it into proposals for fundamental social change. Economists of the mainstream, who came to dominate the development of economics, may have been radical in many other fields, but in regard to economic conditions they remained conservative.

Incidentally, even in modern times we can see how a radically egalitarian doctrine is often stated in particularly ostentatious terms and is seemingly accepted by everybody—in general terms—in countries that are very far from the realization of the ideal expressed in the doctrine. Thus, in the United States the egalitarian principle and, specifically, the quest for equal opportunities are—like other elements of the American Creed—commonly accepted and announced in terms closely resembling the ways of expression of the Enlightenment.

At the same time, this country is backwards as a welfare state. Its social security system, for instance, is incomplete and is molded in the outdated pattern from the time of Bismarck and Lloyd George when this social problem was not yet conceived as one of comprehensive national policies. And the country is suffering from large-scale, pathological poverty and cultural impoverishment in its extensive urban and rural slums. In the very much more advanced countries in Northern Europe, for instance, there is actually much less public oration about equality or even democracy than in the United States while, of course, the people of these countries have more of an egalitarian reality.

Likewise, in a very poor, underdeveloped country like India, with enormous inequalities increasing all the time, the "welfare state," the "classless society," or the "socialist pattern of society" are constantly said to influence planning and all public policies, sometimes with the implication that the country has actually proceeded a long way towards realizing these ideals.

# XXI · *Inhibitions and How They Are Gradually Overcome*

As a political force, this living and, on an abstract level, generally accepted ideal that greater equality is desirable, of course, encountered the vested interests of those who were better off and who would have had to make sacrifices.

Everywhere there has been a chasm between the lofty egalitarian principle concerning the nature of a more perfect society and the very imperfect reality we permit to exist around us. In this uncomfortable situation people have been grasping for rationalizations in order to reconcile with their exhalted ideals their valuations on the lower level that for the most part determine their day-to-day living, including their voting in elections.

In Sections III and IV above, I discussed the struc-

ture of distorted beliefs, stereotypes, and popular theories which become the instruments for people's efforts
to present "reasoned opinions" to themselves and their
surroundings.

One element of these structures is the belief that a
racial group or all poor people are different by nature.
As I pointed out, this belief received certain support
from the naturalist speculations in the Enlightenment
and later from social Darwinism.

Another element is the moralistic idea that the poor
and destitute have themselves to blame for their mis-
fortunes. They have not taken advantage of their
opportunities.

Their intellectual and moral inferiority is generally
considered to be confirmed by common experience. To
counter the inference from such observations, the
social scientists have a general argument: namely,
that the currently observed inferiority in some groups is
itself a result of earlier inequities which repressed them.
But it was opportunistic for people to believe that this
was not the full explanation.

Then there is the idea that reforms for equalization
would hold back economic progress, both by decreasing the incentives for those who had to pay for them
and by decreasing the motivation of the poor to strive,
work, and save when relieved from pressing wants
and insecurity. Even in an advanced country like
Sweden, it was no more than a generation ago that
such arguments were posed by the conservatives against

the social security reforms then being promoted on an increasingly large scale.

The common assumption that redistributional reforms are costly for society as a whole and not only for the rich is apparent in the fact that such reforms have continuously been motivated only in terms of social justice. When, in those countries that have achieved the most in egalitarian reform, the idea has emerged—and in more recent times become confirmed by research—that the reforms have spurred economic progress and thus, from a national point of view, been a profitable investment, as a rule this has been an afterthought.

Finally, but not least important, comes what may be called "the convenience of ignorance." It can be observed that in the compromise thinking and living which is normal when a gross disparity exists between the equality ideal and a social reality characterized by glaring inequalities, people who live in comfortable circumstances have usually succeeded in remaining ignorant of the poverty and distress around them. Ignorance—like knowledge—is seldom random but is instead highly opportunistic, as we have argued throughout this book and illustrated in Section IV.

This last observation may give a clue to an understanding of one reason why the egalitarian idea has, on the whole, been winning and has resulted in social reforms. Empirical social science studies in the great English survey tradition from early in the nineteenth century have undoubtedly played their part. And the spread of embarrassing knowledge has been one of the consequences of the greater articulateness on the part of the poor themselves and of efforts of their political organizations to plead their cause and bring them to fight for it.

For the world at large, the secretariats of the intergovernmental organizations within the United Nations have in the postwar era, through their research and publications, effectively spread information about the great poverty in the underdeveloped countries and the widening income gap between them and the developed countries. Moreover, these same organizations have been utilized by the poor countries to endorse complaints and demands for greater equality.

Meanwhile, in the developed countries, the rise in productivity has given egalitarian reforms more elbow room. People have realized that the reforms did not ruin the economy—as the opponents regularly had forecast—and recently observers have come to understand (with the aid of empirical research) that the greater equality achieved by the reforms was instead actually productive from a national point of view. Consequently, the political possibilities for reforms finally expanded.

As the reform movement gathered momentum and increasing public support under these influences, we have been able to witness how in the most advanced welfare state the political parties have begun to compete with each other in propagating reforms. The State is thus becoming what a Swedish political scientist has called the "Service State," eager to cater to its clients, the citizens.

What is still limiting the pace of this movement is the scarcity of funds as subjectively conceived by the ordinary citizen in even the richest of countries. He is apt to demand more and more of those public undertakings which contain egalitarian reforms—for instance better health and school facilities—yet at the same time he is likely to resist higher taxes or at least a too rapid increase of taxes, and often he demands lower taxes.

These easily explainable but irrational attitudes on the part of the citizenry (wanting much for little) have habitually led even the richest countries—and not least those—to inflation and foreign exchange difficulties or have led them to risk such difficulties. In the United States and to a varying degree in the other rich countries too, the staggering fiscal burden of wars and war preparation and of other public undertakings (such as space programs) of no immediate interest from the welfare point of view have been pressing in the same direction. These influences have acted as a brake, slowing down but usually not stopping the reform movement.

# XXII · *Theoretical Escapism*

The reaction of economic and social theory to the paradoxical situation I hinted at in Section XX can be broadly characterized as one of escapism.

From one point of view, the persistent tendency of economic theory to take special precautionary measures to keep from drawing practical policy inferences from the egalitarian principle at its very basis stands out as a sort of backhanded recognition of the sovereignty of this ideal. In a sense, *the structure of economic theory has been determined entirely by the need to protect itself from its own radical premises.* Contemporary efforts to avoid value-loaded terms by inventing more innocent-sounding ones (Section XII above) testify to this need felt for protection.

Of course, many of the popular theories I referred

to in discussing lay opinions in Section XXI had their counterpart in the writings of the social scientists as well and were thus presented in a more learned form. But there were also a number of other devices lacking comparable equivalents in popular thought.

One such device in the time of classical economics was Malthus' population theory, which made a permanent rise in the standard of living of the masses of people seem unattainable. Malthus' original pamphlet, as well as his later, more comprehensive treatment of the problem, was a part of the general European trend towards conservatism in the aftermath of the American and French revolutions.

More generally, after the egalitarian principle had been "proved," it tended to be confined to an abstract compartment in the basement of economic theory, insulated by impregnable abstruseness. Otherwise, every effort was made in the development of theory to avoid stating problems in such a way that the principle could be used as premise for practical policy conclusions. How the classical economists in their time managed to avoid radical inferences from their radical premises is a question of continuing importance, for the influences under which they were working and the devices they used can often be found operating even today.

One such device was the isolation of the problem of distribution of income and wealth from the sphere of production, including exchange. Though it goes much further back, this distinction was finally developed by John Stuart Mill. In the sphere of production and exchange, natural laws reigned, and policy interventions would only hamper production. Distribution of income and wealth, on the other hand, was the legitimate sphere in which the egalitarian principle was valid.

While "the laws and conditions of the production of wealth partake of the character of physical truths," explains Mill, it was not so with the distribution of wealth. That was "a matter of human institutions solely . . . . The distribution of wealth, therefore, depends on the laws and customs of society" which can be changed.[41]

This distinction is, first, logically untenable as the size of a country's production and its distribution are interdependent and determined within the same macrosystem.[42] But leaving this aside for the moment, the economists used the distinction to direct their interests almost entirely to production and exchange while now and then expressing a general reservation in regard to the distributional problem.

This tendency to avoid dealing with distribution—where the political conclusions derived from the egalitarian principle had been confined—was supported from the beginning by a basic predilection among economists for the old notion of the harmony of inter-

41. *The Political Element in the Development of Economic Theory*, pp. 129 ff. and App., pp. 208–17.
42. *Principles of Political Economy*, 1848, ed. by Ashley, 1903, vol. II, i, 1.

ests and a consequent predilection for *laissez-faire*. This predilection was preserved in economic theory to a much greater extent than uninformed observers realize, and it is often not clearly perceived by the theorists themselves.

I touch here on a very involved matter. In this connection I shall merely point out that the predilection for the doctrine of harmony of interests has also a logical "reason," stemming from the attempt to identify "what is" with "what ought to be." Without the assumption of interest harmony, the theorist would have been required to solve the insoluble problem of how, in actual social accounting, to calculate the maximization of "pleasures" and "pains" in terms of "general welfare."

This identification is at the bottom of the philosophy of natural law as well as of utilitarianism. To begin with, it is the essence of the natural law concept of what is "natural." Though reasoning in a more circumstantial way, the utilitarians could not escape a similar identification when required to explain both actual and rational behavior in terms of "pleasures" and "pains."

The point I want to make is that to the extent that our (usually uncontrolled) reasoning about economic matters comes under the influence of these old and powerful predilections, our attention will regularly be turned away from the problem of equality. Politically, these predilections represent a conservative bias. As I mentioned, there were at all times radical writers who insisted on studying economic and social reality from the point of view of the egalitarian principle. But the main line of development of economic theory was laid out by writers who were inclined to turn their interest away from this issue.


On a more practical plane, the economists in the classical and later neoclassical stream were impressed by the decrease of savings and the disorganization of production that could follow an induced change of distribution. (This implied an indirect concession that the sharp distinction they had observed between the spheres of production and distribution was not logically tenable.)

Thus, Alfred Marshall held that it was "the part of responsible men to proceed cautiously and tentatively in abrogating or modifying even such rights as may seem to be inappropriate to the ideal conditions of social life." He was then expressing a thought that goes far back in history and had already been formulated with particular emphasis by Bentham.

Writing at the time when the welfare state had begun to take form in Britain, Marshall conceded that the earlier economists, when not assuming "responsibility of advocating rapid advances on untried paths," had lacked vision and "in some respects [had been] narrower than . . . most educated men in the present time."

In addition, we must take into account what I have called the "realism of conservatism." A principle of historical selection was at work: the conservatively inclined economists seemed to come nearer an explanation of social reality. This theoretical superiority of conservative thinking is, of course, entirely fortuitous. It does not imply that conservative conclusions are in any sense "true" or even "truer" than the more radical ones. It means only that, because they implicitly applied more conservative valuations, these economists reached policy conclusions which were in closer agreement with the actual power relations of their time—in contradiction to the radical premises at the basis of their theory.

It should be noted that at a later date the economists in the classical line under the influence of the social and political forces at work in our countries generally became less adverse to more radical policies, yet they restricted these policies narrowly to the national community. Alfred Marshall, quoted above as the most open-minded representative of our profession of his time, observed just after the close of the First World War:

"We are indeed approaching rapidly to conditions which have no close precedent in the past, but are perhaps really more natural than those which they are supplanting—conditions under which the relations between the various strata of a civilized nation are being based on reason rather than tradition . . . .

". . . it is becoming clear that this [Great Britain] and every other Western country can now afford to make increased sacrifices of national wealth for the purpose of raising the quality of life throughout their whole population. A time may come when such matters will be treated as of cosmopolitan rather than national obligation: but that time is not in sight. For the practical purpose of the present and the coming generation, each country must, in the main, dispose of her own resources, and bear her own burdens."


Developments in the world at large since Marshall's time have led economists to argue for aid to the underdeveloped countries.

# XXIII · *Conclusion*

Conventional economic theory is still far from having liberated itself from the metaphysical assumptions it inherited from the moral philosophies of natural law and utilitarianism. Nor has our science yet outgrown the devices used to protect it from its own radical premises. This is why an intensive critical analysis—in terms of the type of logic barely hinted at in the preceding section—is of continuing importance.[43]

But when this is accomplished, a great number of problems are open to empirical research.

Why and how did early social scientists—like proponents of the great religions and moral philosophies attached to the religions—adopt and give such a cen-

43. See p. 86, fn. 40.

tral position in their theories to the egalitarian principle?

The escapist tendencies of economic theory in regard to the egalitarian postulate are more easily understandable. They were an adjustment to conditions concerning prevalent valuations and to the political power situation in the countries in which this theory developed. Once one places oneself outside the main trend of economic speculation and looks at the development of theory as a part of social and political history—all of which needs to be explained in terms of causes and effects—there is little mystery about it. Karl Marx—himself involved in the metaphysical preconceptions of the old philosophers, as evidenced, for instance, in his theory of "real value"—never carried out this explanation, although in his empirical, historical, and sociological excursions there are many hints towards such an explanation. These are buried, however, in his teleological doctrine.

The real mystery, which I am not in the position to solve in this context, is the continuous presence in clear form of the egalitarian principle. Where did this lofty ideal come from? And how could it continuously preserve its position at the basis of abstract economic reasoning in Western (and Communist) civilization?

Another problem for empirical research is whether and to what extent the development of the welfare state in the advanced countries was promoted by the position given to the egalitarian principle in all economic thought. Also, what role does this ideological heritage play today in our adjustment in the rich countries to the radically changed postwar political conditions in the underdeveloped countries and our relations to them.

On these questions I would like answers founded upon empirical research, much of it of a historical nature following an institutional approach. Fortunately, I do not need these answers in order to come to terms with the methodological problem raised in this essay.

# INDEX

*About the Author*

Gunnar Myrdal, winner of the 1974 Nobel Prize in economics, is best known in the United States as the primary author of the noted Carnegie study, *An American Dilemma*. He has written many other books, among them, *Challenge to Affluence* and *The Political Element in the Development of Economic Theory*. His wife, Alvah Myrdal, won the Nobel Prize for peace. Their home is in Stockholm.